THE BIRDS OF KILLINGWORTH LAKE

1995 - 2010

HANS STEINER

In memory of my good friend,
Jim Purcell (1935 – 2013)

FOREWORD

This book about the birds of Killingworth Lake in North Tyneside is dedicated to my good friend and former next- door neighbour, Jim Purcell (1935-2013)[1].

For 15 years between 1995 and 2010, we met usually twice a day, morning and evening, to take our dogs, 'Sam' and 'Penny', for a walk from our homes in Elm Grove, about 1 mile from the Lake.

Jenny, Ted and Jim with 'Sam' and 'Penny'

Jim with his
Wife, Kathleen

My interest in watching birds started during my retirement in December 1994, as a consultant paediatrician in Newcastle upon Tyne. We built a conservatory in our new home in Elm Grove in Forest Hall and retained the apple tree that stood at one of its corners, which birds visited frequently, especially after we added feeders to some of the branches and other areas of the garden. I had also long been interested in photography and my first digital camera was presented to me, a few weeks earlier, at my retirement party at the Sunderland Dog Racing Track by Alan Craft, on behalf of friends and colleagues of the Department of Child Health in Newcastle - a Sony 100 alpha camera with 2 Canon lenses, EFS 18 - 55 and 55 - 250. I took the equipment with me twice a day, when Jim, my next door neighbour, and I met with our dogs, 'Sam' and 'Penny" to take them out for a walk to the field close to our house and around the Lake, where I took photographs of all the resident birds and the frequent visitors, for 15 years between 1995 and 2010. Jim had no particular interest in birds, but he was interested in the derivation of their names, their history, particularly during the two World Wars of the 19th century and their mythology, superstitions and folklore. He introduced me to the story from ancient Greece of the union of Zeus, disguised as a swan, to Leda, the Queen of Sparta, during which Helen of Troy was conceived. These interests - beyond the mere identification of individual birds seen on the Lake - have stayed with me since then and are included in this book, in so far as I have been able to collect the information from the considerable literature available in recent years. I am sure that Jim would have appreciated the wonderful collection of books about the lives of some of the birds, which I have been able to collect and record in the Bibliography.

Jim was the best friend I ever had during my adult life. He was a gentleman, kind, considerate and tolerant with a 'laid back' attitude to life.

Killingworth, a town north of Newcastle upon Tyne, was built as a planned new town by Northumberland County Council in 1963, intended for 20,000 people. It was a former mining community of derelict colliery land near Killingworth Village[2].

In about 1964, a lake south of the town centre, was created in the former mining village - spoil heaps were levelled and planted with trees. A main road from Newcastle separates the lake into two areas. Later, the lake was kept well stocked with fish and local wildlife abounded. An angling club and model boating club use it regularly. During our daily walks with our dogs, I took my camera and tripod with me and took photographs of the resident birds and newcomers for 15 years, whilst Jim and I talked about the affairs of the world, literature, jazz, politics, science and much else. At times, my wife, Jenny, accompanied us and used the scope for a better view of the birds on the waters of the lake.

The result is a photographic record, by an amateur bird watcher, of the bird life from nesting to fledging of some of the common birds of our inland artificial lake and the occasional visitors from other areas.

Notes

1. I am indebted to Jim's wife, Kathleen, for the following information: "Jim loved books of all kinds. He loved music, Especially Jazz at which he was an expert - Duke Ellington was a favourite- he was also keen on classical music.

He was an excellent golfer, a life-long member of the Morpeth Golf Club in Northumberland, with a handicap of one, when he first met Kathleen in 1964 and 6 at the age of about 50 years.

He sadly died in a nursing home at the age of 73 years from a brain tumour. There are 3 children from his marriage".

The Purcells were great family friends from the first day of our arrival in Elm Groove. It is a strange and wonderful coincidence that both Kathleen and Jenny met their life-long partners at a dance at the Mayfair night club in Newcastle and both were very happily married within a year of their meeting. All four had never been to a nightclub before. Jim loved dogs and he always had control of them; he could throw the ball prodigious distances for them to catch and bring straight back to him'.

We began our walks in the field about a quarter of a mile from our homes, where we let our dogs free and met other dog-walkers, notably Paul and his two sheep dogs 'Meg' and 'Marge' and Ted with his lovely Airedale, 'Peggy'. We then moved on to circulate around the Lake. My wife, Jenny, joined us from time to time and joined Jim at regular intervals in patrolling the field and collect the rubbish that accumulated there. She liked to watch the birds with us.

2. The Killingworh colliery had one of the world's most famous pits, where in 1814, George Stephenson, engine wright at the colliery, built his first steam driven locomotive, *Blucher*, with the help and encouragement of his manager, Nichols Wood, in the colliery workshop behind his house, "Dial Cottage", which is close to our home in Elm Grove in Forest Hall. This locomotive could haul 30 long tons of coal up a hill at 4mph. It was used to tow wagons of coal from Killingworth to the Wallsend staithes. The engine, however, did not survive long but it provided Stephenson with the knowledge and experience to build better locomotives at Killingworth, including the famous 'Rocket', in his locomotive works in Newcastle.

References

Wikipedia: Killingworth
                George Stephenson

Note: All the photographs except those on page 54 and 87 were taken by me with my camera.

SWANS

The English word "swan" is derived from the Proto-European root "swen' - to make sound. Thus, it is related to Old English "geswin" - melody, song and "swinsian" - to make melody.

Note: the roots of the reconstructed Proto- Indian-European. Language (PIE) are basic parts of words that carry a lexical meaning, so-called morphemes PIE roots.

'Lexical' means relating to the words of a language.

THE MUTE SWAN

1

Why are some swans mute, in comparison with all the other, strongly vocal swans of their species, including the trumpeter, whooper and tundra swans?

The all have an extremely elongated trachea, which uniquely convolutes within an opening in the sternum to emerge and link up with the bronchi to the lungs via a syrinx (a fluid filled cavity) and tympanic membranes. As a result, the increased length and air chamber volume provide enhanced resonating and harmonic potential for vocalising.

The mute swan has only a short trachea, like most vertebrates, and only manages hisses and snorts when threatened or excited.

Due to relatively limited vocalisation, its territories are correspondingly small and in some protected places, mute swans even form dense nesting colonies, crammed with up to 100 birds. This is not the case in Killingworth Lake, where I estimate that the number of adults and juvenile is usually of the order of 40-

The photograph on the preceding page is unique in that there were at the time, no less than 24 birds crammed into one corner of the lake.

The Royal Society for the Protection of Birds (RSPB) had brought some mute swans in their big white van for sanctuary, rest and rehabilitation following periods of distressed living conditions in parts of the North-East of England. They remained there for variable periods of time and then flew away to other destinations. Extra food in the form of grain was provided for them.

FLIGHT

The swan, at an average weight of 10kg, is the heaviest bird that flies and thereby expends a great deal of energy to become airborne, following a relatively long 'run-up' on the water. The seemingly effortless flight following take off, is dependent on a complex balance of forces.

Thrust which pushes the bird forwards and upwards has to be greater than the air resistance, which pulls the bird back as it flies. Thrust is provided by the downward stroke of the wing, whereas the upwards stroke overcomes the air resistance, which is further reduced by a slight folding of the wings which improves the aerodynamics of the flight.

The wings are curved at the top and flat along the bottom. Thereby the air travels a longer distance as it passes over the top of the wing and this, in turn, reduces the pressure above the wing and increases the air pressure below the wing, creating the lift, which pushes the bird upwards and enables it to fly. Once airborne, the swan continues to flap its wings slowly and intermittently to keep it moving, as it spreads its large wings to make the maximum use of the air currents and glide with the minimum of energy expenditure.

Basically, there are two features, which are all important. These are the lightest possible weight and the most efficient intake of oxygen to provide and maintain efficient metabolism to sustain the energy required for flight, notably the take-off and the landing. The wings, feathers and body have a complex structure to maximise the ability of the bird to keep flying. The weight is kept at the lowest possible point by the hollow structure of the bones, which are filled with air and the network of air sacs throughout the body, which fill with air at each breath. As a result, the bird absorbs 100% of inhaled oxygen with each breath, compared with only 20% in humans. The plumage is so structured as to minimise air resistance, improve the streamlining and the aerodynamics, and reduce the amount of energy needed to move through the air.

The landing on the water is tricky. The swans have to use their webbed feet as paddles to skid awkwardly to a halt.

Swans are almost entirely herbivorous, Mute swans eat both fresh-water or salt-water plants such as pondweeds, musk grass, eel grass, algae, roots tubers and stem leaves of aquatic and submerged plants. Occasionally they also catch small aquatic animals, including small fish and frogs.

They feed mainly by up-ending, so that they end up with their bottoms at right angle to the water. They can reach several feet beneath the surface.

A pair of black swans visited the lake and stayed for a few days. I managed to obtain a photograph of only one on its own. They are native to Australia and New Zealand and were brought to Britain some years ago and may be found in the collections of many waterfowl reserves.

REPRODUCTIVE BIOLOGY

Pair formation and bonding begins with mutual "greeting ceremonies", including head turning and bonds are firmly established through "triumph ceremonies". Pre-copulation displays consist of mutual preening with the neck feathers ruffled.

The female is mostly concerned with the nest building during the Spring (March to June), but the male helps.

The nest is relatively large, about one meter in diameter and eggs are usually laid every other day for 5 to 6 days and sometimes longer.

The nest consists of rushes, reeds, herbaceous vegetation and sticks. It is lined with soft down and feathers.

The mother incubates the eggs for 35-45 days, before the chicks hatch one by one on successive days,

They stay close to her in the area by the nest until they have all hatched and follow her into the water. This strategy has evolved in order to help her to cope better.

By then their eyes are open and they are able to swim and beginning to feed independently.

The male stands guard during the incubation period and for a short while as the mother and the chicks take to the waters. He does not to take any further part in rearing the brood and starts to compete with other males in order to mate with new partners.

The cygnets leave the nest the day after hatching. They remain close to the parents, often riding on their backs for a while before entering the water.

The fledging period lasts for four and a half months. The cygnets usually remain close to their parents until severe weather conditions force families to return to winter quarters and merge with larger groups of swans.

Typically, the young of the past year are thrown out of the territory by their parents before the latter start breeding again. In the meantime, they swim in linear formation attended often by both parents.

The record for longevity in captivity is 21 years. Juveniles have brown patches on their bodies, which diminish after 12 to 14 months, when they are physically mature and begin reproductive behaviour.

Surprisingly, some nests are at times adjacent to the main road separating the two lakes, in close proximity to people and dogs on leads, such as Jim's dog, "Sam", on one occasion, and to traffic. The swans do not seem to be disturbed in these surroundings. But male swans, guarding the nest and the family, may exhibit dangerous aggressive behaviour, when people and dogs come into too close proximity to them.

A young mute swan

A pair of bonded mute swans. A fully mature white male with a large black knob on the forehead, with a juvenile female, physically mature and smaller than the male; but with the retention of brown patches on her body, only about 1 year old and thereby most unlikely to be fertile - she will usually have to wait until she is 2 to 4 years old before she is able to conceive. The classic "heart shaped posture" is usually associated with post-copulative behaviour (although sometimes seen before copulation) with touching and rubbing of heads and neck, rhythmical movements from side to side and nodding of heads.

Aggressive attack postures of male mute swans

The male is significantly taller, heavier and more aggressive than the female.
He also has a much larger knob on the forehead.

21

A cycle race of 10 Km around the larger of the two lakes was held in the winter. There were usually a dozen or so competitors.

I entered the race on one occasion with my mountain bike but gave up after two laps of the course. I just could no longer cope with sharp incline at the start of each circuit.

MALLARD

The name is derived from the Old French word 'mallart' or 'malari' meaning wild drake. The name can also be traced to the German 'Madelhart', a common name for males at the time. Also to English words 'Mawdelard' or 'maudelard' used as adjectives.

Like the growth and hardening of a buck's antlers, drake mallards acquire their brightly coloured feathers, legs, and bill in response to an increase in testosterone. These hormonal changes are triggered by decreasing day length in late summer. Ducks begin to pair up in the autumn and because drakes must compete for less numerous hens, they develop their breeding plumage as early as their body condition allows. Being fat and brightly coloured gives drakes a decided advantage over smaller and less conspicuous males. Age and nutrition can influence when a drake mallard develops breeding plumage. Older males tend to ramp up their testosterone level faster than younger ones. No matter the age of the drake, however, he needs to have access to an abundance of high-quality food to fuel this seasonal transition.

For hens, acquiring a strong, healthy mate is crucial. During winter, females must feed heavily to acquire enough nutrients to complete the winter moult and to prepare for the rigours of the spring migration and breeding season. Having a mate by her side allows her to feed without being interrupted while the drake watches for predators and wards off competing pairs.

After selecting a mate and spending the winter together, the hen leads her drake back to the area where she was hatched. It is the hen that has a strong homing instinct, and the drake is only along for the ride.

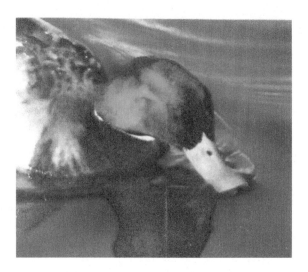

Mallards on the frozen waters of Killingworth lake, with a
solitary pochard 2nd from the right.

RESIDENT – The Heron, a solitary bird; usually standing motionless for hours on end at the water's edge on the smaller of the two lakes, ready to pounce on fish in the water and passing youngsters.

Mallard with one or two Moorhens on the grassy verge of the lake is a common sight. The reasons is probably that they both feed on the grass and insects on the verges of the lake.

THE DUCKS ON KILINGWORTH LAKE
– RESIDENTS AND VISITORS

RESIDENT – Tufted Duck

RESIDENTS – Cormorants

RESIDENTS – Moorhen

A Flock of Canada Geese flying over the lake

RESIDENT – Canada Geese

The resident solitary Heron flew over the bigger lake to stand at the water's edge there.

Visitors - White ducks (one of the numerous mutations of ducks).

Muscovy ducks, male on the left and female on the right.

VISITORS – Golden Eye – with gull and goosander

A Female Golden Eye

VISITORS - Pochards

VISITOR – Little Grebe

VISITORS – Common Mergansers; female standing at the edge of the lake.

Pair with Male on left and Female on the right

The mergansers were sufficiently rare on Killingworth Lake for twitchers to gather at the edge of the lake in 2008 with their cameras and scopes to observe two pairs of the mergansers* It was reported that there were only 6000 breeding pairs in the whole of Britain.

The photograph was taken some time in June 2008, when all the males were about to migrate to Norway, leaving the females to care for the young on her own.

Female mersanger

Caring for her youngsters

Photographs from Image Credits –istockphoto.com

RESIDENTS – Coots. There were three nests

Floating nest of coots, within close proximity to the heron standing guard on the smaller lake

Coot's nest jutting out from the side of the larger lake

Coot's nest on an artificial island close to the side of the larger lake

GULLS are often in the sky above the lake or in the water, alongside the other birds.

Black Headed Guls

The reason for the abundance of seabirds on Killingworth Lake is the close proximity of the coast of Tyne and Wear and Northumberland to the North. The driving distance between Killingworth and Whitley Bay is just over 5 miles.

VISITORS - Terns

VISITOR – A single Raven on a wall by the lake.

VISITORS – Brent Goose alongside Canada Goose

A Warbler – Possibly Willow

A Sand Martin flying over the lake

VISITORS – Swifts

Swifts seldom come to rest on land, except to feed their young.

SWIFTS – Resting on the fence

VISITORS – The white pied wagtail

GREAT CRESTED GREBE – from nest building to fledging

GREAT CRESTED GREBE – Courtship ceremony

Photograph from Nature Magazine – "How grebes walk on water". J. Exp. Biol. 1235 – 1243 (2015)

The heaviest animals known to run on water pull off the feat by using quick strides and large feet that slap the surface.

Western and Clark's grebes (Aechmophorus occidentals **and** Aechmophorus clarkii; **pictured**) run as far as **20 metres** on water and for up to **7 seconds** during a mating ritual, and are among only a few animals with this ability. Glenna Clifton at Harvard University's Concord Field Station in Bedford, Massachusetts, and her team analysed high-speed video of wild birds performing the dance and studied models of the grebe foot in the laboratory.

They found that the birds stay above the water by having a fast stride rate of up to **20 steps a second**, as well as wide, flat feet that slap the water surface with enough force to support up to 55% of the bird's weight. The animal's feet are also shaped to reduce drag.

The eggs hatch one at a time over a period of 24-48 hours, and the young stay on the nest close to the mother until they have all hatched. This system has evolved in order to help her and for the safety of her brood.

The latter all take to the water and begin to feed independently, when all have hatched.

The male remains close to them all, fishing to help the young and guarding the family.

Jenny at Killingworth Lake in 2008

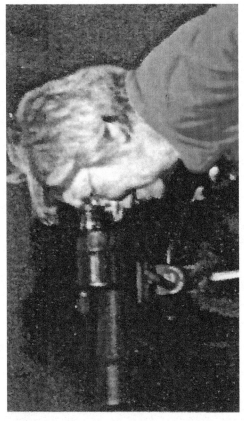

Mythology, Superstition and Folklore

Swans

"The swan's grace, serenity and white feathers give it the appearance of an almost otherworldly creature. This meant that in many traditional legends in Europe, swans appear both as maidens and youths under enchantment. Similarly in folk belief Swans were thought to represent the souls of the dead who were pure of heart, and so it was considered very bad luck to kill them or harm them.

Niall MacCoitir

In England, swans have a special cultural value as a royal bird. Many streets, hotels and especially pubs (there are more than 700) are named after them. It occurs often in heraldry; the principal device on the badge of Henry V was a silver swan.

The swan was a prestige food for the aristocracy in the time of Queen Elizabeth I.

It went out of favour because it was too flavoursome and because of the rise of popularity of turkey from the 16th century onwards. In Tchaikovsky ballet, *Swan Lake,* based on a German legend, a beautiful maiden called Odette is forced into the form of a swan by a wicked magician, Von Rothbart.

She has a human form only at night and can only fully regain it through the power of eternal love from a man, who will remain faithful to her. Odette and a young prince called Siegfried fall in love. The magician tricks Siegfried in being unfaithful with his daughter Odile, who is a double of Odette. Siegfried is full of remorse and because their love can never be realised, Odette and Siegfried choose to die together rather than be parted and throw themselves into a lake.

In the Classical myth, Orpheus, the musician became a swan and the swan was said by the ancient Greeks to be a bird of Apollo, the god of music.

Legends, myths, folklore and superstitions about swans abound throughout the ages and many countries in the world. They are often a symbol of fidelity and love due to their long-lasting monogamous relationships. They feature in Wagner's operas, Lohengrin and Parsifal.

In classical literature, there is a belief that that the mute swan would sing beautifully upon death - hence the "swan song".

The best-known children's story is the fable of "the Ugly Duckling".

It is recorded in 1986 in the Scots magazine (July 440) that fishermen in the Dornoch Firth area believe that the swan is a portent of bad luck.

W.B. Yeats, the Irish poet wrote *"The Wild Swans of Coole"*, focusing on the "mesmerising" characteristics of the swan and retells the legend of Leda of ancient Greece in the same poem. Swans are revered in Hinduism and are compared to saintly persons, whose chief characteristic is to be in the world without getting attached to it, just as a swan's feather does not get wet although it is in water.

A swan is one of the attributes of Saint Hugh of Lincoln, based on the story of a swan which was devoted to him.

The black swan *(Cygnus atratus)*

Is widely referenced in Australian culture, although the character of that importance historically diverges between the prosaic in the East and the symbolic in the West. The black swan is also of spiritual significance in the traditional histories of many Australian Aboriginal peoples across southern Australia. Metaphoric references to black swans have appeared in European culture since long before Europeans became aware of *Cygnus atratus* in Australia in the 18th century. The black swan is the official state emblem of Western Australia and is depicted on the flag of Western Australia, as well as being depicted on the Western Australian coat-of-arms. The symbol is used in other emblems, coins, logos, mascots and in the naming of sports teams. The arrival of the black swan in Europe brought the birds into contact with another aspect of European mythology. The attribution of sinister relationships between the devil and black coloured animals, such as the black cat. They were associated with witches and often chased away and killed by superstitious folk.

This may explain why black swans have never established a strong presence as feral animals in Europe or North America.

Heron

The Greek myths refer to the heron as the messenger of God, so they never harmed a heron because they believed it would bring bad luck upon them. Stories of Athena tell us that one of her messengers was a heron. Heron is also symbolic of virtue and honour.

In Ancient Greek art, the heron plays a vital role in striking a balance in the continuous struggle between evil and good.

The Egyptians too, shared a profound relationship with this beautiful bird because a God named Bennu was a large gold and red heron. Heliopolis, one of Egypt's oldest cities, considered this bird highly sacred. Bennu was the creator of light, which is why the city came to be recognized as the city of the Sun.

The heron spirit animal has a variety of messages pertaining to us humans. One message it delivers to us is independence. By nature, humans are either too social or too solitary and the heron teaches us that we do need each other but only to a particular extent. The solitary characteristic of the heron also teaches us not to be so overly social that we lose our own distinct individuality and identity in the crowd.

The heron is a symbol of the wonders of nature and independence. The white heron shows us how it needs to be protected against the destructive forces of greed and industrialization. In China, the people wear the heron tattoo as a sign of longevity, patience, purity, and strength.

The Africans considered the heron as a communicator with God, so a heron tattoo for them has a highly sacred meaning and depicts a profound relationship they might share with the gods. If anyone apart from these cultures wears the heron tattoo, the most common interpretation of it would be of a statement of their intention to improve their status.

People may also associate the heron tattoo as a signal to let the person wearing it remain in their state of tranquillity and stillness and not to interfere too much into their quiet peace.

Conclusion.

The heron symbolism speaks primarily of solitude and loneliness but in a positive light. It shows how individuals can live on their own and not complicate their lives with too much interference and involvement of other human beings.

1593, Nashe *Christs Tears over Jerusalem 90.* "The Vulgar mentality conclude, Therefore, it (the plague) is like to encrease, because a Hearnshow (this English surname also refers to Heron). A whole afternoon together, sate on the top of St Peter's Church in Cornhill".

1932. C. Egglesden. *"Those Superstitions 79".* In the marshlands of England the heron was never shot for fear of ill luck". 1949. S. P. B. Mais *"Who dies? 240 (Wales).* "As we drew up at the door of the hotel at Maes-yr-Afon, I saw a heron fly slowly over the house, that bird of ill-omen to travellers".

1960. K. Stewart Croftinthe Hills. *164 9. (Loch Ness Inverness).* "There are intangible legacies from the past. A neighbour of ours, young and active and full of fun, will look anxiously at a heron, bird of ill omen, flapping his way from the hill, lest he should pass too near her place".

Cormorants

Many cultures consider cormorants a symbol of nobility and indulgence. In more recent history, the cormorant is considered a good luck charm for fishermen, or a talisman that will bring a fisherman a bountiful catch.

In China and Japan, humans once exploited the fishing skills of the cormorant by tying a snare to the bird's throat and sending it to sea. The snare prevented the bird from swallowing fish, and when the bird returned to the fisherman's boat, the fisherman removed the fish and kept it.

Some specific stories of cormorants in literature include

> In the Greek tale of Ulysses, after a storm broke the mast of Ulysses' raft, a sea nymph disguised herself as a cormorant and handed Ulysses a girdle to keep him afloat while he swam to shore.
> In Norwegian myths and folklore, three cormorants flying together are said to be carrying messages and warnings from the dead. In northern Norway, cormorants are considered to be good luck when they gather in a village. Norwegian myth also states that people who die at sea can visit their former homes in the form of a cormorant.
> In Polynesian mythology, Maru-tuahu used feathers to make himself "as handsome as the crested cormorant" when both young daughters of Te Whatu declared their desires to marry him.
> In Ireland and some other places, seeing a cormorant perched atop a church steeple is a warning of bad luck to come.
> In England, the mythical "Liver Bird," the symbol of the city of Liverpool, is thought to be a cross between a cormorant and an eagle.

In some Scandinavian areas, cormorants are considered a good omen; in particular, in Norwegian tradition spirits of those lost at sea come to visit their loved ones disguised as cormorants. The cormorant is also a symbol of greed and deception in John Milton's epic poem, *Paradise Lost,* as the form Satan took to disguise himself to enter Eden before tempting Eve.

Muscovy Ducks.
Aztec rulers wore cloaks made from the feathers of the Muscovy Duck, which was considered the totem animal of the Wind God, Ehecatl.

Native American Mudhen (Coot) Mythology
Coot plays the role of Earth-Diver in some Native American tribes, being the only animal to succeed at diving to the ocean floor to bring up earth for the Creator or culture hero to make the world with. Coots, also known as mudhens, are also used as clan animals in some Native American cultures. Tribes with Coot Clans include the Menominee tribe (whose Coot Clan is named Kihkih.)

Native American Legends About Coots

Kawaiisu Flood Myth:
Legend of the Kawaiisu tribe of California, in which Coot dives for dirt to help Coyote rebuild the earth after a flood.

Waynaboozhoo and the Great Flood:
Version of the Ojibwe creation story in which Mudhen (Coot) retrieves land for the culture hero Nanabozho.

Remaking **the** Earth: A Creation Story from **the** Great Plains of North America:
Picture book based on Cheyenne and Blackfoot Indian creation myths in which Coot takes on the role of Earth-diver.

Birds of Algonquin Legend:
Interesting collection of Native American legends about coots and other birds in Algonquian tribes.

Birds Of Fancy
A good book on the meaning of birds in world mythology, including Native North America.

Native American Animal Stories:
American Indian tales about animals, told by Abenaki storyteller Joseph Bruchac.

Sea birds
Seabirds were thought to carry the souls of dead sailors and it is considered bad luck to kill one.

Ravens.

Like other black birds, the raven (an attendant to the gods of both ancient Greece and Scandinavia) is widely considered a creature of ill omen. It is feared for its apparent ability to foresee death.

A raven is particularity disliked around the sick because their cries sound like "corpse, corpse." It is believed that a raven around someone sick is an omen that the patient will not recover. Scientists suggest that the association with death has to do with a raven's strong sense of smell, which draws it to decaying flesh.

In the olden days, the raven is said to be the favourite disguise of the devil. And eleventh century Norman invaders used ravens as their emblem, which made the bird a harbinger of war. But according to Welsh tradition, if a blind person shows kindness to a raven, it will help that person regain his or her sight. They also welcome the sight of a raven on the roof of the house because it is said to bring luck to everyone within.

In the West Country, ravens are saluted by the raising of the hat, and anyone who robs a raven's nest is said to be punished by the death of a baby in his or her home village. Similarly, the Cornish warn against harming a raven, explaining that the bird may be the reincarnation of King Arthur.

The royal connection is expanded in London, where it is said that the British monarchy and the United Kingdom itself will last only so long as there are ravens at the Tower of London. This well-known superstition is thought to have evolved from the story of Bran the Blessed, a mythical figure whose head is said to be buried on Tower Hill facing France to ward off any invasion of England. The name Bran means raven. And anyone who kills one of the ravens that live in the Tower will soon die too.

A relatively obscure tradition allows a person to get information about the future by counting ravens. If one raven is seen, sadness is in store. If two are spotted, happy days lie ahead. If three ravens are counted, there will be a marriage. And if four ravens appear, there will be a birth. A variation, however, claims that it is only lucky if one raven is seen, and unfortunate to see any more. In the business of weather prediction, ravens flying towards the sun are a sign of fine weather. If they are preening themselves on the wing, it means there will be rain. Should they fly recklessly into one another, it means war is coming.

C40 BC. Virgil *Eclogue IX.* "If a timely raven on my left hand...had not warned me at all costs to cut short this last dispute, neither your friend Moeris nor Menalcas himself would be alive today".

AD 77. Pliny *Natural History XXV (*1855 II 492). "Ravens... are of the very worst omen when they swallow their voice, as if they were being choked".

1507. *"Gospelles of Dystaues pt. 3V.* "Whan the lorde or the lady of a house is seke, and that a rauen cometh and cryeth vpon the chambre, whereas the payent lyeth, it is synge that that he shall deye of that sykenes".

1587 Gifford *Subtill Practises of Devilles Cl-2.* The raven he siteth upon the steeple and cryeth, which way dot he looke sayeth one, from thence ye shal haue an eie ere it be long".

1606. SHAKESPEARE. "The raven himselfe is hoarse. That croaks the fatall entrance of Duncen Under my battlements".

C. 1650. Dr Wren Note in Browne's Vulgar Errors V XIII (1852, II 79). "The raven by his acute sense of smelling discerns the savour of the dying. And that makes them flutter about the windows, as thy use to doe in the searche of a carcass ...

thence ignorant people counte them omnious, as foreboding deathe, and in some kind as causing death.

1693. *Athenian Mercury 1 April,* "here's a raven has built a nest in the North-west Pinnacle of Louth Church...the like has not been remembered for 60 years and above. Some people look upon it as Ominous".

1748. SMOLLETT Roderick Random XIII. "at that instant a monstrous, overgrown raven entered our chamber...and made directly towards our bed. As this creature is reckoned in our country a common vehicle for the devil and witches to play their pranks in, I verily I believed we were haunted, and, in a violent fright, shrunk under the bed-clothes.

1799. Southey *Poems II.* 'Old Woman at Berkeley'. "The Raven croaked as she sate at her meal. And the Old Woman knew what he said. And she grew pale at the Raven's tale. And sickened and went to her bed".

1853. *N & QIst ser. VII496.* "At an ordinary meeting of the guardians of the poor...the officer stated that the applicant's inability to work was due to depressed spirits, produced by the flight of a croaking raven over her dwelling on the morning of his visit'.

1873.. Kilvert *Diary 26 May.* "John Vincent said that a man was sick at Derry Hill. Two ravens flew over the house crying 'Corpse, Corpse'. The man died the next day.

1899. *Weekly Chronicle* 11 February 7 (Jesmond). "The Cheviot shepherds say they hear the raven laugh when someone is about to die".

1910 HUDSON *Shepherd's Life X.* "He had much to say about the old belief that the raven 'smells death', and when seen hovering over a flock, uttering the croak, it is a sure sign that a sheep is in a bad way and will shortly die".

1922 R. KEAARTON. *At Home* with *wild Nature 58-9.* "In the Highlands of Scotland even educated people have a dread of the bad luck a raven is likely to bring them. I remember...entering s friend's house with the wing quill of one of these birds in my hand, and be seriously entreated to dispose of it at once lest it should bring one of us misfortune".

1932 J. M. SAXBY *Shetland Lore 123.* No raven had croaked within hearing (of the bridal party). The young couple were to be happy all their lives |

1971 *Trans Devon Ass. 268* (Stockley Pomeroy). "A croaking raven (not a rook) was a sign of coming bad luck. Mr Brown adds that he has found this to be true.

That if a martin's nest is destroyed on a farm, the cows will give milk tainted with blood.

Swifts

1866 (N & Q 3rd ser, Xii 203 Isle of Thanet, Kent). The farmer said, "Knock them back swifts down, sir, they are regular wings of the devil... the martins and swallows...bring good luck. Them black imps bring the contrary".

The imp is a small mischievous devil.

Ibid 271. Almost all the provincial names of the swift seem to indicate something unholy, as Devling, Deviler, Sker-devil, Screech devil.

1883 *Folklore* 194 (Hants). "A farmer who made light of popular superstition went out one day, by way of bravado, shot seventeen swifts. He was the owner of seventeen fine cows, but before seventeen weeks were over every one of his cows died.

1885 Swainson *British Birds* 95 (Yorks) "It is called Devil Bird."

1889. *Folklore* 44, Moray. If the 'black swallows'... are out, there will be no luck.

SWIFT FOLKLORE

It took a long time to fully understand the natural history of the swift.

Jenner (already famous for his work on cowpox and smallpox vaccination) marked some Swifts by cutting their toes off (well at least he knew they had some!). He found that they returned to the same place to breed in a fattened and healthy condition and was more than ever certain that his theory of migration was correct.

A French Airman in the 1914-18 war was gliding down in his plane with engines turned off so as to avoid detection when at 10,000 feet he found himself amongst birds which were apparently motionless. One of these birds was found the following day caught in the engine and found to be a Swift. Moving on many years to 1947 and the renowned ornithologist David Lack began watching Swifts in Oxford and this became one of the longest such projects in the world and which continues to this day. In 1956 this resulted in the classic book *Swifts in the Tower.*

Perhaps the most persistent myth of all is that Swifts are closely related to Swallows and Martins. The truth is this is just a trick of convergent evolution and the Swift's closest relative is actually the New World humming birds and the South Asian tree swifts.

Martins

1787 *Provincial glossary* Superstitions 65. "It is deemed lucky to have martins or swallows build their nests in the caves of a house, or on the chimneys".

1827 HONE *Everyday Book II 19 Nov.*"It is considered a presage of good for (a martin) to build its nest in the corner of the bedroom window and particularly so, should the first inhabitants return in the season.

1863 R. CHAMBERS *Book of Days* 1 678 (Suffolk), "It is lucky for you that martins should build against your house. They will never come to one where there is strife. Soon after setting up housekeeping for myself, I was congratulated on a martin having built its nets in the porch over my front door.

1878 *N & Q* 5th ser x 65. "There is a curious superstition in Cheshire that if a martin's nest is destroyed on a farm, the cows will give milk tainted with blood".

1928 E. LOVETT *Surrey and Sussex* 16. "It is unlucky o destroy martins' nests in a house".

1938 *Folklore* 91 (Shelfanger Norfolk). "The farmer's wife wanted some house-martin's nests removed, as they were soiling the window-sills The man employed in painting, however, said his master had warned him not to injure the nests as it was very unlucky, and he had known a man break his leg after having done so".

1978 A. WRIGHT. *Holderness* 14 (E. Yorks). If house martins build on your home, a baby will come.

Goose myth

One version of the myth about the barnacle *{Branta "anas" leucopsis)* and brant *("Branta bernicla")* geese is that these geese emerge fully-formed from goose barnacles. There are other myths about how the barnacle goose breeds. The basis of all the myths is that the bird, *"Branta leucopsis"*, emerges and grows from matter other than bird eggs. There are many sources to the myth. The etymology of the term "barnacle" suggests Latin, Old English and French roots.

There are references in pre-Christian books and manuscripts-some Roman or Greek. Further reference can also be found in an earlier pre-Christian period. The main vector for the myth into modern times was monastic manuscripts and in particular the "Bestiary".

The myth owes its long-standing popularity to an ignorance of the migration patterns of geese. Early medieval discussions of the nature of living organisms were often based on myths or genuine ignorance of what is now known about phenomena such as bird migration.

It was not until the late 19th century that research showed that such geese migrate northwards to nest and breed in Greenland or northern Scandinavia.

An early, but not the first references to the myth of the barnacle goose is in the eleventh century Exeter Book of Riddles.

The riddle is asked as follows:

"My beak was close fettered, the currents of ocean, running cold beneath me. There I grew in the sea, my body close to the moving wood. I was all alive when I came from the water clad all in black, but a part of me white. When living the air lifted me up, the wind from the wave bore me afar - up over the seal's bath.

Tell me my name...." to which the anticipated answer was: 'The Barnacle Goose'.

The 12th-century bishop Giraldus Cambrensis was one of the first to put the legend to paper, in his *Topographia Hiberniae*. The notion that a male goose could spontaneously spring forth from a tree was, in his view, irrefutable evidence of the Immaculate Conception of Christ. Two centuries later, the myth reappeared in the popular book *The Travels of Sir John Mandeville*, published around 1356:

"I told them of as great a marvel to them, that is amongst us, and that was of the Bernakes. For I told them that in our country were trees that bear a fruit that become birds flying, and those that fell in the water live, and they that fall on the earth die".

Throughout the Middle Ages, the myth of the barnacle goose and the goose barnacle "fruit" thought to give birth to it, retained a hold on religious culture. A few Irish clergy saw a loophole in the rule that forbade eating meat of the flesh (any meat other than seafood) during fasting. The "tree-goose", being spontaneously generated from a plant, was fair game.

For Jewish rabbis the issue of whether to eat the birds at all became a serious question. Some rabbis strictly prohibited their consumption, on the grounds that the birds were "vermin" (though whether they were land vermin or flying vermin was open to debate). More liberal rabbis who thought they could be eaten wondered whether, upon consumption, the goose should be blessed as a bird or a fruit.

Goosander

For the native American Ojibway people, the goosander or common merganser was a symbol of resilience and fortitude.

In legend, the bird used these qualities to withstand the harsh winters of the Northern states of the USA.

Ducks

Throughout history, the image of ducks is almost universally benign -with one exception. In the 13th century, when the Stedinger people of Friesland a province of the Netherlands resisted the dominance of the German powers around them, Pope Gregory IX (c. 1145 or before 1170-22 August 1241) wrote letters denouncing the rebels as worshipers of the devil, who appeared sometimes in the shape of a goose or a duck, the Stedinger were massacred, yet the charge was obviously absurd - a duck devil could never ring true.

For the southern Zuni people of the USA, ducks were the form which spirits took when travelling home.

The Zuni are Native American Pueblo peoples native to the Zuni River valley. The current day Zuni are a Federally recognised tribe and most live in the Pueblo of Zuni on the Zuni River, a tributary of the Little Colorado River, in western New Mexico, United States.

The birds were also linked to fertility.

Duck Christianity Symbolism

What does a duck symbolise in the Bible? The way it presents itself to become waterproof is linked to anointing in Christianity, a symbol of blessing, protection and enlightenment. In the Bible, people were named to king or prophet status, as a symbolic gesture for God's gift. It is unclear whether the Bible considers the duck's meat clean or unclean, for it states that swans should not be eaten, and some believe that ducks are included.

A Christian story depicts a little boy playing with a slingshot and killing his grandmother's duck. Scared, he hides the body, but his sister sees him, keeps the secret, but manipulates him into doing all of her chores. In the end, the boy is tired of being a slave, so he confesses to the grandmother.

She reveals that she already knew from the beginning and already has forgiven him.

The duck symbol is used in this story to illustrate God's love and Satan's enslavement.

A duck superstition

In 1604, *Depositions, York Castle* 23 July (1861, 127n). Office against Katherine Thompson and Anne Nevelson. "Pretending to be charmers of sick folks, that they used to bring white live ducks or drakes and set the bill thereof to the mouth of the sick person, and mumble up their charms in such a strange manner as damnable and horrible".

To sum up - The Wonder of Birds

"Legend has it that storks bring babies, doves are holy, crows evil, vultures rapacious, while across the world, eagles are symbolic of power.

Why since the birth of time, have birds been such a source of fascination that successive cultures have developed their own avian myth, legend, folklore and superstitions, and conferred on their native species human and often superhuman traits?

It is in their appearance, voice and behaviour that so many stories and beliefs have originated. Colour has helped to decide whether a bird is 'good' (white) or 'bad or evil' (black), much the same way that Christian symbolism paints angels and devils. Similarly, birds with haunting calls are widely associated with death".

Through the accounts of different species, a glimpse is given of the mythology, legends, folklore and superstitions of the birds that were seen and photographed on Killingworth Lake in North Tyneside.

References

Steve Madge and Hilary Burn (1988). "Waterfowl. An identification guide to the ducks geese and swans of the world". Houghton Mifflin Company.

Paul Johnsgard (2016). "Swans: Their Biology and Natural History". Zea Books. University of Nebraska-Lincoln. Wikipedia: Swan (contains a good, comprehensive account of the mythology associated with them).

A. Lindsey Price (1940) 'The Swans of the World. In nature, history, myth and art". Council Oak Books

R.H.J. Brown (1963). "The flight of birds". Biological Reviews. Volume 38, Issue 4/pp, 460-489

(Note: includes information related to the flight of swans - the heaviest of the birds that fly).

Abby Daniele (2017) Seagull. An Educational children's Book". (Note: Includes mainly photographs of the common species). Peter Hayman and Rob Hume.

(2005). "The Pocket Guide to the Coastal Birds of Britain and Europe". Mitchell Beazley. Michael Brooke (2008). "Far from Land. The mysterious lives of seabirds" Princeton University Press.

"The Goosander". A group of black and white photographs of these interesting birds, printed by Amazon. (No information about author(s).

From The Natural History Museum Library (1991). "Ducks. A selection of prints from the Museum's wildlife publications. Julian Huxley (First published in 1914 and reprinted in 1968). Note: The publication of the first ecological study of birds. David Lack (2018). "Swifts in a Tower". Unicorn Publishing. Note: interesting insights in the swifts' private lives). Homing experiments on swifts deprived of olfactory perception in Italian Journal of Zoology Volume 8, 1974- Issue 4. Published online 12 July 2013.

"The Courtship Habits of the Great Crested Grebe". Jonathan Cape. (Note: This is the first published ecological field study of a bird species).

K. E. L. Simmons (1989). "The Great Crested Grebe". Shire Natural History Series. Copyright K. E. L. Simmons.

K. L. L. Simmons (1955. Published for the Avicultural Society), "Studies on Great Crested Grebes'. Reprinted from the Avicultural Magazine Vol. 61, 1955.

Chapter: Duck Pp. 12-15 in "Rachel Warren Chad and Marianne Taylor (2016). "Birds, Myth, Lore & Legend". Bloomsbury Natural History.

Edward Giles (2018). "Those with Webbed Feet. All about British ducks, geese and swans". Brambleby Books.

Joe Shute (2018)."A Above. The fall and rise of the raven". Bloomsbury,

Wikipedia: Swan; Mallard; Hero; Canada geese; Tufded ducks; Cormorants; White ducks; Muscovy; Pochards; Rook; Brent goose; Golden eye; Warbler; Sand Martin; Swifts; White Pied Wagtail; Little Grebe; Gulls; Black Headed Gull; Tern; Great Crested Grebe.

Also in Wikipedia: Friesland; Pope Gregory IX; Zuni people.

"Amazing Facts about Swifts". RSPB.

Books and papers about the Mythology, Superstitions and folklore of birds

Iona Opie and Moira Tatem (1989). "A Dictionary of Superstitions". Oxford University Press. Niall Mac Coitir (2015). "Ireland's Birds. Myths, Legends and Folklore". The Collins Press.

Rachel Warren Chadd and Marianne Taylor 2016). "Birds. Myth, Lore and Legend". Bloomsbury.

Bibliography - for general background reading

Walter Steak (1910) A Concise Etymological Dictionary of the English Language" American Book Company.

Killian Mullarney, Lars Svenson, Dan ZetterstrOm, Peter J. Grant (1999). "Bird Guide". The most complete, field guide to the birds of Britain and Europe. Collins Press.

Stephen Moss (2018) "Mrs Moreau's Warbler. How Birds got their names". Guardian Faber. UK and USA.

Samuel Fanous (2014). "A Conspiracy of Ravens, A compendium of collective names for birds". Bodleian Library.

Simon Webb (2016). The Parliament of Fowls by Jeffrey Chaucer. In a Modern English Translations. Probably written by Chaucer in 1382

R.S.R.Fitter and R.A. Richardson (1954). "Pocket Guide of Nests and Eggs. The complete identification book". Every British nesting bird illustrated. Collins.

Colin Tudge (2008). "The Bird. A natural history of who birds are, where they come from, and how they live". Crown Publishers. New York.

John Rilley (2018). "The ascent of birds. How modern science is revealing their story", Pelagic Publishing.

Tim Birkhead (2008). "The Wisdom of Birds. An illustrated history of Ornithology". Bloomsbury. Note: Includes an interesting Chapter on "Sex". Pp.273-299.

Jennifer Ackerman (2016). "The Genius of Birds". Corsair.

Paul D. Sturkie (1954). "Avian Physiology". Comstock Publishing Associates.

Madeleine Floyd. (2ol0). "Birdsong". National Trust.

John Long and Peter Schouten (2008). "Feathered Dinosaurs. The origin of birds". CSIRO Publishing.

John J. Videler (2005). Avian Flight. Oxford University Press. Simon Barnes (2006).

Henk Tennekes (2009). "The Simple Science of Flight".

From Insects to Jumbo. JEB. The MIT Press.

The Wildfowl and Wetlands Trust, the aims.

Note: includes many photographs of their birds in the wetlands.).Noah Strycker (2014). "The Thing with feathers. The surprising lives of birds and what they reveal about being human". Riverhead Books. Jim Al-Khalili and Johnjoe McFadden (2014). "Life on the Edge. The coming of age of quantum biology". Transworld Publishers. Gordon Corera (2018).

"Secret Pigeon Service. Opration Columba. Resistance and the struggle to liberate Europe". William Collins. Note: Jim would have appreciated this book about birds in World War II)

"How To Be a Bad Birdwatcher. To the glory of life". Short Books Giorgio Bassani (1968).

"The Heron". A NOVEL (Note: An excellent book to read at bedtime or other convenient time).

Izzi Howell (2020). Citizen Scientist. Studying Birds. Wayland. Niall Edworthy (2009).

"Bald Coot and Screaming Loon. A handbook for the curious bird lover". Eden Project Books

Printed in Great Britain
by Amazon